Let Freedom Ring

# The Early American Industrial Revolution, 1793–1850

by Katie Bagley

**Consultant:**

Melodie Andrews, Ph.D.
Associate Professor of Early American History
Minnesota State University, Mankato

Bridgestone Books
an imprint of Capstone Press
Mankato, Minnesota

**Bridgestone Books** are published by Capstone Press
151 Good Counsel Drive, P.O. Box 669, Mankato, Minnesota 56002
http://www.capstone-press.com

*Library of Congress Cataloging-in-Publication Data*
Bagley, Katie.
    The early American Industrial Revolution, 1793–1850/by Katie Bagley.
    p. cm.—(Let freedom ring)
    Summary: Follows the development of the American Industrial
Revolution from 1793 to 1850, including the major industrial inventions
and advances of the time period.
    Includes bibliographical references and index.
    ISBN 0-7368-1557-0 (hardcover)
    1. Industrial revolution—United States—Juvenile literature. 2. Industries—
United States—History—Juvenile literature. 3. United States—Economic
conditions—To 1865—Juvenile literature. [1. Industrial revolution—United
States. 2. Industries—United States—History. 3. United States—Economic
conditions—To 1865.] I. Title. II. Series.
HC105 .B13 2003
330.973'05—dc21                                         2002010826

**Editorial Credits**
Angela Kaelberer, editor; Kia Adams, series designer; Juliette Peters,
    book designer; Angi Gahler, illustrator; Kelly Garvin, photo researcher;
    Karen Risch, product planning editor

**Photo Credits**
Bettmann/Corbis, 22
Corbis, cover (main)
Henry Ford Museum & Greenfield Village, 41
Hulton/Archive by Getty Images, 10, 42
Maryland Historical Society, 32
North Wind Picture Archives, cover (inset), 13, 15, 16, 19, 27, 30, 37, 38, 43
Stock Montage, Inc., 5, 6, 9, 21, 25, 35

1   2   3   4   5   6   08   07   06   05   04   03

# Table of Contents

# Chapter One

# The Early American Industrial Revolution

In 1851, the Great Exhibition took place in the Crystal Palace in London, England. This event was the first World's Fair. People from many countries brought their best products. Great Britain was the world's most industrialized country, but it was the Americans who amazed everyone.

Compared to the number of entries, the United States won more prizes than any other country. The judges gave awards to American revolvers, rifles, and other weapons. American farm machines, rubber products, and even a dried meat biscuit received major awards.

People were amazed that a young country like the United States had won so many awards. After the fair, British experts came to the United States to study American manufacturing methods.

In 1851, more than 6 million people viewed the 13,000 exhibits at the Great Exhibition in the Crystal Palace in London, England.

# Different Views

After the United States won independence from Great Britain, some Americans wanted the new country to industrialize quickly. In 1791, Secretary of the Treasury Alexander Hamilton, pictured below, spoke to the U.S. Congress. He explained the advantages of industrializing. He said it would create more jobs and help the United States be less dependent on Great Britain.

Thomas Jefferson and Benjamin Franklin did not agree with Hamilton. They thought the United States would be stronger if the country stayed a nation of farmers. They thought that living in cities and working in factories was unhealthy.

## A New World Power

The United States had not always been an industrial leader. In the 1700s, most Americans were farmers. The United States bought nearly all of its manufactured goods from Great Britain. The early American Industrial Revolution is the process that changed the United States into an industrial power.

At first, Americans copied British industrial methods. But Americans soon thought of better ways to produce goods faster and more cheaply. Americans built new kinds of factories. They invented tools and machines. They built thousands of miles of canals, roads, and railways to move goods and supplies across the growing nation.

The Industrial Revolution changed lives in the young nation. Some Americans became wealthy owners of factories or mills. Some Americans became inventors and engineers. Others worked long hours in dangerous factories or mines. By 1900, the United States was the leading industrial nation in the world.

# Chapter Two

# Beginnings in Great Britain

The Industrial Revolution began in Great Britain during the late 1700s. Progress came with new sources of power, new machines for making cloth, and new ways of making iron ore into metal.

## Steam Power

In 1698, British inventor Thomas Savery developed the first useful steam engine. Steam engines burn wood, coal, or other fuel to turn water into steam. The steam supplies the power to turn the parts of the engine.

In the 1760s, Scottish engineer James Watt improved the steam engine. He added a part that cooled the steam and changed it back into water. This condenser allowed Watt's engine to use much less fuel than earlier steam engines had used.

James Watt built a steam engine that used less fuel than earlier steam engines did.

Watt's engine could power many kinds of machines. Before the steam engine, cloth factories relied on water to power machinery. These textile mills had to be built on rivers or streams. Watt's engine allowed mills to be built anywhere.

## Textile Inventions

Other inventors improved the textile industry. Before the Industrial Revolution, people worked in their homes to spin cotton, flax, and wool into thread by hand. They used looms to weave the

James Hargreaves invented the spinning jenny. The machine helped Great Britain become the world's top producer of cloth.

thread into cloth. A part called a shuttle held the thread. Weavers used their hands to move the shuttle from one side of the loom to the other.

British inventors created machines that could work much faster than people could. In the 1730s, John Kay invented the flying shuttle for the loom. This shuttle moved automatically, allowing a weaver to work twice as fast. In 1764, James Hargreaves invented the spinning jenny. This machine could spin eight threads into cloth at once. Five years later, Richard Arkwright discovered how to use water for spinning power. His machine was called a water frame. It produced stronger thread than the spinning jenny did.

Samuel Crompton invented a machine in 1779 that used the best features of the spinning jenny and the water frame. The machine was called a mule. It produced fine, strong thread.

In the late 1700s, Great Britain's textile industry began to use more spinning and weaving machines powered by water or steam. Great Britain led the world in producing cloth.

## Coal and Iron

The iron industry was important to Great Britain's growth as an industrial nation. The country was rich in iron ore deposits.

Before iron could be used, the metal had to be removed from the ore. People used a furnace to melt the ore and separate the liquid iron from the rock. This process is called smelting.

Before the early 1700s, charcoal made from wood was the main fuel used for smelting. Britain also had large underground deposits of coal. Coal was cheaper, more plentiful, and burned better than charcoal. In 1709, Abraham Darby discovered a way to use coal to smelt iron.

In 1784, Henry Cort found a way to produce a purer form of iron. Cort also invented new ways to shape iron into useful forms. By the late 1700s, many factory and farm machines were made of iron. Iron also was used to build ships and bridges.

Coal furnaces smelted iron ore, separating the liquid metal from the rock. By the late 1700s and early 1800s, many machines, ships, and bridges were made of iron.

# Chapter Three

# Technology Crosses the Atlantic

Great Britain did not want other countries to copy its inventions. The British government outlawed the sale of machines to anyone outside the country. The government also passed laws to stop mechanics and engineers from leaving Britain.

Americans wanted to learn how British inventions worked. They invited British mechanics to come to the United States. Some Americans even offered money to people with knowledge of the latest methods and machines. Many skilled workers found ways to get around the British laws. These workers moved to the United States.

## Samuel Slater's Mill

In 1789, a young man named Samuel Slater left Britain for the United States. Slater had worked for eight years in a cotton mill in Derbyshire, England.

Samuel Slater's mill in Pawtucket, Rhode Island, still stands today.

Slater worked for Jedediah Strutt, who was a business partner of Richard Arkwright. At the mill, Slater used Arkwright's textile machinery. He learned how to build the spinning frames. When he left Britain, Slater told British officials that he was a farmer, so they would allow him to leave the country.

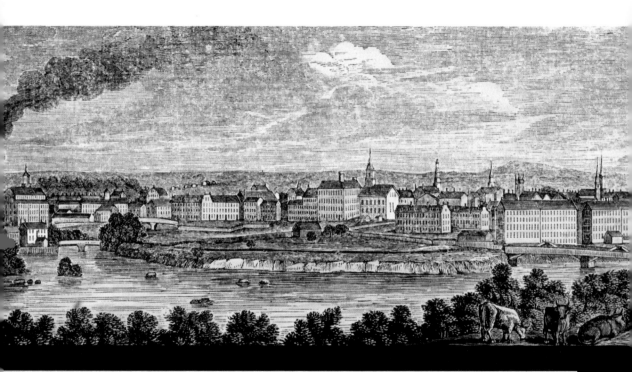

The city of Lowell, Massachusetts, is shown in the 1830s. The city was built around the area's textile mills.

Slater moved to Rhode Island. He found mechanics, builders, and business owners willing to help him pay for and build a mill.

In 1790, Slater completed his mill in Providence, Rhode Island. It was the first successful textile mill in the United States. Three years later, Slater built another mill in Pawtucket, Rhode Island. He later built mills in other New England towns. Many people consider Slater the founder of the cotton textile industry in the United States.

After 1790, many small mills were built in Rhode Island and Massachusetts. Most early mills were built near rivers. Water supplied the power for the mills. Later mills had coal-powered steam engines. These mills did not need to be located near rivers.

## Lowell Mills

In 1810, American businessman Francis Cabot Lowell visited textile mills in Lancashire, England. Two years later, he returned home to Waltham, Massachusetts, to build his own factory.

In 1814, Lowell opened the Boston Manufacturing Company near the Charles River.

His factory was one of the first to include all the machines and processes for making cloth in one building.

## Factory System

Lowell's plan for running his mills became known as the factory system. This system was popular with business owners. Locating all the machines in one place saved both time and money. Each worker performed only one task. This division of labor also helped the mills work faster. Workers were able to produce much more cloth in the same amount of time.

Other people copied Lowell's ideas. Several mills were built north of Waltham on the Merrimack River. In the 1820s, a city developed around the mills. The city was named after Lowell.

Most workers in the Lowell mills were young women from nearby farms. The women lived in dormitories near the mill. The mill had a school for the workers. Workers even published a magazine called *The Lowell Offering*.

# Mill Workers

Mill workers led hard lives. They often worked 12 or 13 hours each day for low wages. When business was slow, owners sometimes made the workers take pay cuts. Workers spent their days in noisy and dangerous conditions. Factory machines were sometimes unsafe. Some workers lost arms, legs, or eyes in factory accidents.

Many mill workers were women and children. Samuel Slater's first mill hired children as young as age 7. Owners paid children even less than they paid adults. Children who worked in factories received little or no schooling.

In 1834, the Lowell mill owners cut the workers' pay. In protest, 800 Lowell workers walked off their jobs. This strike was the largest up to that time. Within a week, most of the workers had returned to their jobs, even though their demands had not been met. Strikes at New England mills continued during the 1830s and 1840s.

# Chapter Four

# Important Inventions

The War of 1812 (1812–1814) was important to American industry. The United States was at war with Great Britain, so British manufactured goods were not readily available. Americans built factories and mills to make their own goods.

## The American System

Eli Whitney gave American manufacturing an important boost. Whitney is best known for his invention of the cotton gin in 1793. This machine quickly removed seeds from the raw cotton.

Whitney also is credited with developing a successful system of interchangeable parts in 1803. Before this time, one worker made all parts of an item by hand. Whitney used machines to produce the different parts.

In one day, Eli Whitney's cotton gin could do the amount of work that before had taken 50 people to do.

Each worker made many identical copies of one type of part. At the end of the process, the different parts were put together to form the item. This mass production of interchangeable parts became known as the American System.

Whitney used his system to make guns called muskets for the U.S. government. People later used the American System to make clocks, shovels, guns, sewing machines, and farming equipment.

Samuel Colt used Eli Whitney's system of interchangeable parts to make his Colt revolvers. Whitney's son, Eli Whitney Jr., designed the machines for Colt's factory in Hartford, Connecticut.

# Patents

Government documents called patents give an inventor the right to produce and sell the invention for a certain number of years. During that time, no one else can make or sell the invention.

## The Colt Revolver

In the early 1830s, Samuel Colt invented a handgun that could be fired several times without reloading. The pistol had a revolving cylinder that contained five or six bullets. Colt called his pistol a revolver. Colt patented the revolver in 1836.

Colt started a company called the Patent Arms Company. Colt used machines to make the revolver parts. Workers then put the parts together to make the guns. At first, Colt was not successful. In 1842, the Patent Arms Company went out of business.

Four years later, the United States went to war with Mexico. The U.S. government ordered 1,000 revolvers from Colt for the Mexican War (1846–1848). Colt built another factory in Hartford, Connecticut. Colt revolvers still are made today.

## The Sewing Machine

British inventor Thomas Saint patented the first sewing machine in 1790. Many people made improvements to Saint's design.

American inventor Elias Howe invented the first lockstitch sewing machine. He patented it in 1846. This machine used two threads to sew a strong stitch called a lockstitch. Soon after, American Isaac Singer invented a similar machine. Howe sued Singer and won. Singer had to pay Howe money earned from his invention. But Singer did not give up. He patented other improvements to the sewing machine. He also developed a system to mass-produce the machines.

By 1854, Singer's company was the largest manufacturer of sewing machines in the world. The company still makes sewing machines today.

## The McCormick Reaper

Not all of the Industrial Revolution's changes happened in factories. In 1831, Virginia farmer Cyrus Hall McCormick invented the first successful machine for cutting ripe grain. He called it a reaper.

One farmer using a tool called a sickle could harvest one-half acre (.2 hectare) of grain in one day. With the reaper, two farmers could harvest 12 acres (5 hectares) in one day.

In 1847, McCormick moved to Chicago, Illinois. He started a factory to mass-produce the reapers.

In 1851, McCormick demonstrated his reaper at the Great Exhibition in London. Judges voted it one of the top five inventions at the fair.

At first, Cyrus Hall McCormick made only a few of his reapers to sell to farmers in Virginia. He later built a factory in Chicago to mass-produce the machines.

# Chapter Five

# Transportation

In the late 1700s, the United States did not have a good transportation system. Manufacturers needed a better way to get supplies and move finished goods to buyers.

## Riverboats

Rivers connected many towns in the United States, but not all boats could travel on rivers. Boats needed to have flat bottoms to travel across shallow parts of the rivers. The boats also needed a dependable source of power.

Several people built riverboats with steam engines in the late 1700s. Their owners did not earn enough money to stay in business.

American artist and engineer Robert Fulton succeeded where others had failed. Fulton made an agreement with the state of New York.

Robert Fulton built a steamboat called the *Clermont* (front) that traveled nearly twice as fast as sailboats at that time.

State officials agreed to let Fulton have all the steamboat business on the Hudson River for 20 years. In return, Fulton had to build a steamboat that could travel 4 miles (6 kilometers) per hour.

In August 1807, Fulton's steamboat, the *North River Steamboat of Clermont*, traveled from New York City to Albany, New York. By sailboat, the 150-mile (240-kilometer) trip took about four days. The *Clermont* made the trip in only 32 hours, traveling almost 5 miles (8 kilometers) per hour. Fulton patented his design and built more steamboats. The boats carried both passengers and goods.

## Roads

In the late 1700s, people built crushed-stone roads called turnpikes. Travelers paid a sum of money called a toll to use the roads. The money was used to maintain and improve the roads.

By the early 1800s, many settlers were moving west of the Ohio River. They needed a good road. In 1806, Congress passed a law to fund a national

# The National Road

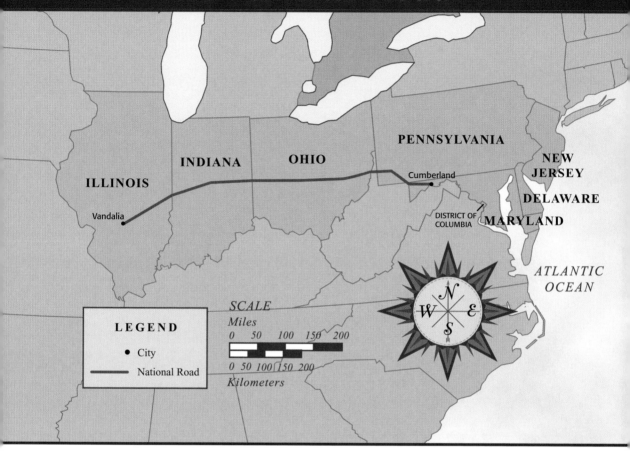

turnpike. Construction began in 1811. When the road was finished in 1852, it stretched more than 500 miles (800 kilometers) from Cumberland, Maryland, to Vandalia, Illinois. The National Road remained the main route west until railroad travel became more common.

# The Erie Canal

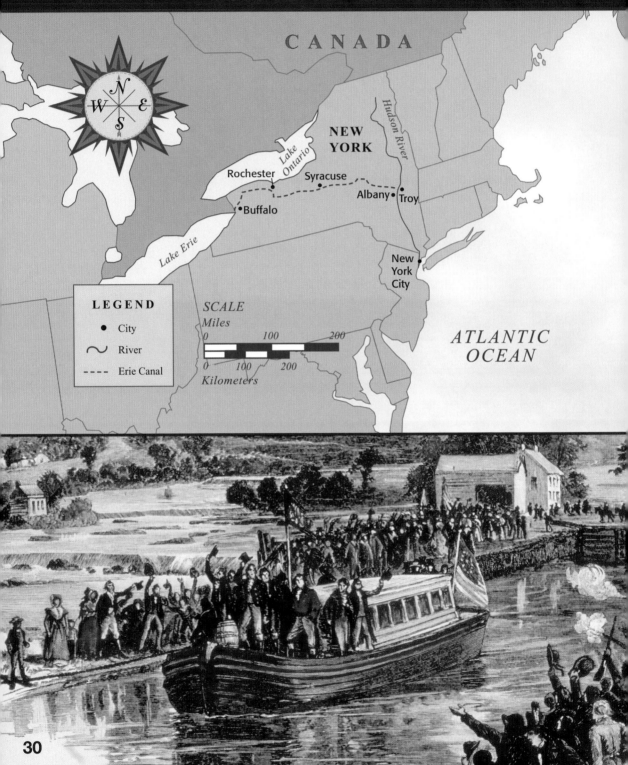

# Canals

Turnpikes were better roads than the earlier dirt paths. But snow and mud sometimes made travel difficult on the turnpikes. People needed a better way to transport goods.

People began to build waterways called canals. The Erie Canal was one of the most important. It connected the Hudson River in New York to Lake Erie. The canal allowed ships to travel from the Atlantic Ocean directly to the Great Lakes. Work began on the Erie Canal in 1817. The canal was 363 miles (584 kilometers) long when it was finished eight years later.

Canals offered a cheap way to ship goods. In 1810, the cost to ship 1 ton (.9 metric ton) of freight from Buffalo, New York, to New York City was $100. After the Erie Canal was finished, the cost dropped to less than $10. By 1840, the United States had more than 3,000 miles (4,800 kilometers) of canals.

# Railroads

The first trains were carts pulled by horses or mules along wooden tracks. British inventors added steam power to trains. In 1804, engineer Robert Trevithick designed a steam-powered railroad engine. In 1829, George Stephenson improved Trevithick's design. Stephenson's train, the Rocket, reached a top speed of 29 miles (47 kilometers) per hour.

Within a year, people built trains that could travel more than 40 miles (64 kilometers) per hour. But most early trains could not travel that fast when loaded with freight. Curving track also slowed down the trains.

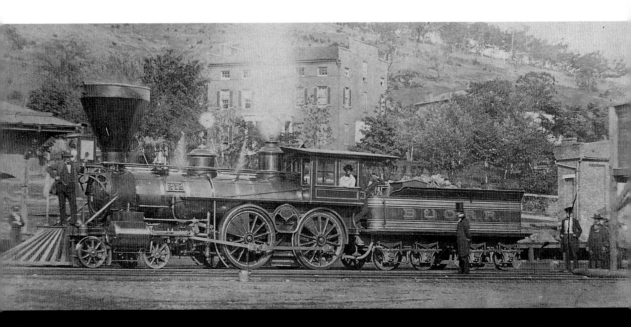

The Baltimore & Ohio (B&O) Railroad, shown here in 1857, was the first railroad built in the United States.

## American Railroads

The first American railroad lines were short. Built in Maryland in 1830, the Baltimore & Ohio (B&O) line was only 13 miles (21 kilometers) long. At first, the railroad used horses to pull its trains. In 1831, it began using steam-powered trains.

The early American trains could not travel fast. In 1832, trains traveled about 6 miles (10 kilometers) per hour. This speed still was faster than canal boats, which traveled about 4 miles (6 kilometers) per hour. Ten years later, U.S. trains traveled at 15 miles (24 kilometers) per hour.

As trains became faster, Americans built more railroads. In 1840, the United States had about 3,000 miles (4,800 kilometers) of tracks. By 1850, that number had tripled.

The railroads helped industrialize the western United States. The open grass plains of the Midwest were suited to raising cattle. By the 1830s, major meatpacking centers were located in Chicago, Illinois; St. Louis, Missouri; Louisville, Kentucky; and Cincinnati, Ohio. Railroads shipped meat produced in the Midwest to the eastern states.

## Morse's Telegraph

The railroad created the need for better communication. To keep railroad schedules and shipments on time, people needed a way to communicate quickly across long distances.

In 1836, Samuel Morse invented a machine called a telegraph. The machine sent electrical signals along a wire. He also invented a code to use with his telegraph. Morse code is a series of short and long electrical signals that stand for letters and words.

The U.S. government paid Morse $30,000 to build a telegraph line between Baltimore, Maryland, and Washington, D.C. On May 24, 1844, Morse sent the first telegraph message, "What hath God wrought!" Soon, people sent messages and money orders long distances by telegraph. Newspaper reporters used the machines to send stories to their offices.

By 1848, all eastern states except Florida had telegraph service. Most telegraph lines followed the railroad tracks.

Samuel Morse's telegraph allowed people to communicate quickly over great distances. By 1861, telegraph lines connected the nation.

# Chapter Six

# Effects of Industrialization

Industrialization did not affect all parts of the country in the same way. The Northeast and Midwest developed most of the industry. The South remained agricultural.

Southern states grew most of the cotton that New England mills made into cloth. The cotton mills' success created a demand for more cotton. Many people were needed to produce the cotton. Plantation owners filled this need with African American slaves.

## Industrialization and the Civil War

The different effects of industrialization helped to separate the two parts of the country. The North and the South had different cultures. They disagreed about many things. One of these issues was slavery.

Most textile mills were located in Northern cities. These mills made cloth from cotton grown in the South.

Many white Southerners thought slavery was necessary to their economy. They saw Northern attempts to limit slavery as an attack on their way of life. Many Northerners thought slavery was an

African American slaves use a cotton gin on a Southern plantation. Plantation owners believed they needed slaves to grow cotton at a profit.

# Tariffs

Taxes on goods produced in other countries and sold in the United States are called tariffs. With tariffs, imported goods sell for higher prices than similar goods produced in the United States.

In the early 1800s, many Northerners believed tariffs would allow new U.S. industries to develop and grow. Supporters also believed tariffs would protect the new industries from competition from other countries.

Most Southerners were against tariffs because they added to the price of goods imported from other countries. Southerners also feared that other countries might add tariffs to the cotton they bought from the United States. Other people thought tariffs might make other countries refuse to trade with the United States. Even today, people still disagree about tariffs.

outdated system. They believed slavery would prevent the nation's economy from growing.

As the United States grew, disagreements over slavery became worse. Slavery was not the only cause of the Civil War (1861–1865). But slavery caused disagreements that were too great for the two sides to work out their problems peacefully.

# Wage Slavery

Some Southerners argued that slavery was better than the "wage slavery" of the Northern factories. Of course, factory owners did not own their workers. But the workers' living and working conditions often were harsh. In factories, people often worked 14-hour days, six days each week. Workers could be fired if they were sick and could not work.

## An Industrial Power

By the 1850s, the United States was an industrial power. By 1900, the United States was the leading industrial nation in the world. People from all over the world bought American goods.

A second Industrial Revolution began in the United States in the late 1800s. Henry Ford's automobile assembly line and other new production methods allowed factories to produce goods more quickly. Americans developed new processes for making steel and refining oil. They also found new ways to use chemicals and electricity. These new inventions and processes all worked together to again change American industry.

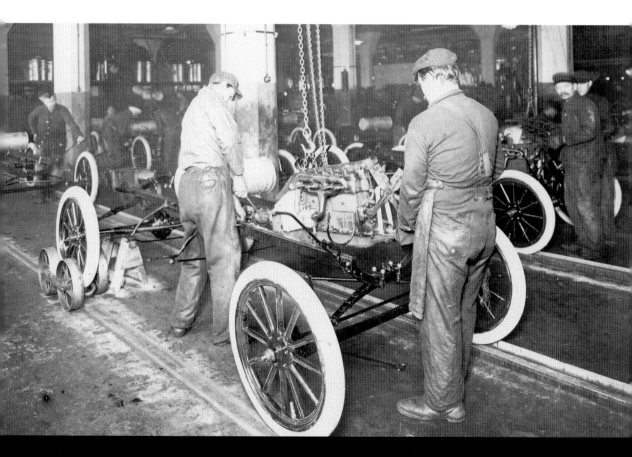

Henry Ford's assembly line allowed cars to be mass-produced at a low cost. By the early 1900s, cars had become the main form of transportation in the United States.

# TIMELINE

Samuel Slater builds a
textile mill in Rhode Island.

The United States and
Great Britain fight the
War of 1812.

The steamboat *Clermont*
makes its first journey.

| 1790 | 1793 | 1807 | 1811 | 1812–1814 | 1825 |

Eli Whitney invents
the cotton gin.

Construction begins on
the National Road.

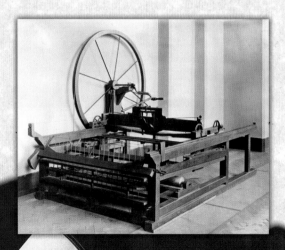

The Erie Canal
is completed.

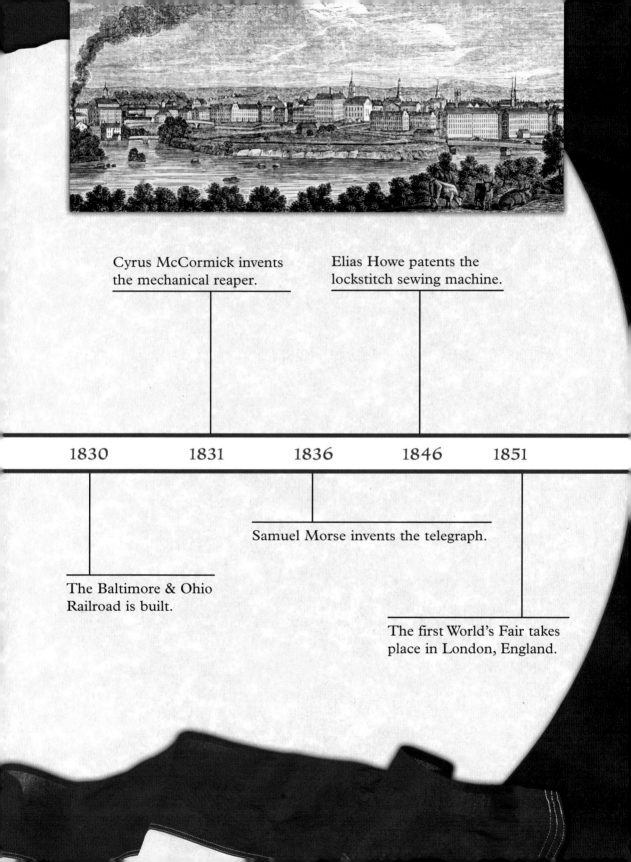

Cyrus McCormick invents
the mechanical reaper.

Elias Howe patents the
lockstitch sewing machine.

| 1830 | 1831 | 1836 | 1846 | 1851 |

Samuel Morse invents the telegraph.

The Baltimore & Ohio
Railroad is built.

The first World's Fair takes
place in London, England.

# Glossary

**canal** (kuh-NAL)—a channel dug across land to connect two bodies of water

**manufacture** (man-yuh-FAK-chur)—to make something, often with machines

**mass production** (MASS pruh-DUHK-shuhn)—a method of making identical products in large numbers

**ore** (OR)—a rock that contains metal

**patent** (PAT-uhnt)—a legal document that gives an inventor the right to make, use, or sell an invention for a set period of years

**smelt** (SMELT)—to melt ore so that the metal can be removed from the rock

**strike** (STRIKE)—a refusal to work until a set of demands is met

**tariff** (TA-rif)—a tax placed by a government on imported goods

**textile** (TEK-stile)—a fabric or cloth that has been woven or knitted

# For Further Reading

**Aldrich, Lisa J.** *Cyrus McCormick and the Mechanical Reaper.* Greensboro, N.C.: Morgan Reynolds Publishing, 2002.

**Bagley, Katie.** *Eli Whitney: American Inventor.* Let Freedom Ring. Mankato, Minn.: Bridgestone Books, 2003.

**Collier, Christopher.** *The Rise of the Cities, 1820–1920.* The Drama of American History. Tarrytown, N.Y.: Marshall Cavendish, Benchmark Books, 2001.

**Collins, Mary.** *The Industrial Revolution.* Cornerstones of Freedom. Danbury, Conn.: Children's Press, 2000.

**Pierce, Morris A.** *Robert Fulton and the Development of the Steamboat.* The Library of American Lives and Times. New York: PowerKids Press, 2003.

**Sproule, Anna.** *James Watt: Master of the Steam Engine.* Giants of Science. Woodbridge, Conn.: Blackbirch Press, 2001.

# Places of Interest

**Eli Whitney Museum**
915 Whitney Avenue
Hamden, CT 06517-4036
This museum is on the site of
Whitney's gunmaking factory,
where he perfected the system of
interchangeable parts.

**Erie Canal Museum**
318 Erie Boulevard East
Syracuse, NY 13202
At this museum, visitors can see a
replica of a canal boat and learn
about the construction of the
Erie Canal.

**Lowell National
Historical Park**
67 Kirk Street
Lowell, MA 01852
The park includes mills, canals,
worker housing, and working
loom machinery.

**McCormick Farm**
Highway 606
P.O. Box 100
Steele's Tavern, VA 24476
The farm includes a blacksmith's
shop, McCormick's house, and a
working grain mill.

**Slater Mill Historic Site**
67 Roosevelt Avenue
P.O. Box 696
Pawtucket, RI 02862
At this site, visitors can see
Slater's original mill, a mill
cottage, and working machinery.

# Internet Sites

**Do you want to learn more about the Early American Industrial Revolution?**
Visit the FACT HOUND at *http://www.facthound.com*

**FACT HOUND** can track down many sites to help you.
All the FACT HOUND sites are hand-selected
by Capstone Press editors. FACT HOUND will fetch the best,
most accurate information to answer your questions.

**IT IS EASY! IT IS FUN!**
1) Go to *http://www.facthound.com*
2) Type in: 0736815570
3) Click on "FETCH IT" and
   FACT HOUND will put you
   on the trail of several helpful links.

You can also search by subject or book title. So, relax
and let our pal FACT HOUND do the research for you!

# Index